W9-AXQ-962

EDGE BOOKS™

FULL THROTTLE

TUNER CARS

by
Jeff Savage

Content Consultant:
Sergiu Mezei
Auto4tuning.com

CAPSTONE PRESS
a capstone imprint

Edge Books are published by Capstone Press,
151 Good Counsel Drive, P.O. Box 669, Mankato, Minnesota 56002.
www.capstonepub.com

 Books published by Capstone Press are manufactured with paper
containing at least 10 percent post-consumer waste.

Library of Congress Cataloging-in-Publication Data
Savage, Jeff, 1961-
  Tuner cars / by Jeff Savage.
    p. cm.—(Edge books. full throttle)
  Includes bibliographical references and index.
  Summary: "Describes tuner cars, including their history, design, and the
competitions and events tuner car owners take part in"—Provided by publisher.
  ISBN 978-1-4296-4750-2 (library binding)
  1. Hot rods—Juvenile literature. 2. Automobiles—Performance—Juvenile
literature. I. Title. II. Series.

  TL236.3.S28 2011
  796.72—dc22   2010000065

Editorial Credits
Carrie Braulick Sheely, editor; Matt Bruning, designer; Laura Manthe,
    production specialist

Photo Credits
Alamy: Photos 12, 4, Richard McDowell, cover, Transtock Inc./E. John Thawley
III, 10, 18; Auto Imagery, Inc., 28; Dreamstime: Mb2006, 24, Mccarthy Studio,
20; Getty Images Inc./Photoshot/Keystone/Alan Band, 8; Newscom: Universal
Pictures, 7, Universal Pictures/Eli Reed, 13; Ron Kimball Stock/Ron Kimball, 15,
16, 17, 22; Shutterstock: Luciano Meirelles, 26, Luciano Meirelles, 26, 29, Maksim
Toome, 6, Max Earey, 14;Wikimedia Commons/Morio, 27

Artistic Effects
Dreamstime: In-finity, Michaelkovachev; iStockphoto: Michael Irwin, Russell
Tate; Shutterstock: Els Jooren, Fedorov Oleksiy, javarman, jgl247, Marilyn Volan,
Pocike

Printed in the United States of America in Stevens Point, Wisconsin.
052011   006196R

Table of Contents

STARS OF THE BIG SCREEN

The 2001 movie *The Fast and the Furious* was a blockbuster hit. In one of the most unforgettable scenes, Brian O'Conner's 1995 Toyota Supra lines up next to Dominic Toretto's 1970 Dodge Charger. Both drivers stomp on their gas pedals, revving their cars' engines. When the light turns green, the cars blast off like rockets. The Charger does a huge wheelie and gets a lead on the Supra. But after Brian uses his nitrous oxide kit, the race becomes a head-to-head battle. In the end, Brian wins when Dominic's Charger crashes.

Brian O'Conner's Toyota Supra (front) was the second car that he drove in the movie. His first was a Mitsubishi Eclipse.

Brian's Toyota Supra and cars like it are the superstars of *The Fast and the Furious* movies. These action-packed movies pushed tuner cars into the spotlight. But tuner car builders were working behind the scenes before the first movie hit the big screen. In garages across the United States, they **customized** cars part by part. Their goal? To have the meanest, fastest cars around.

Fast Fact: The story of *The Fast and the Furious* continued with more movies. The fourth movie was released in 2009.

customize—to change a vehicle based on the owner's needs and tastes

TUNERS IN ACTION

To see tuner cars in action, you don't have to go to the movie theater—just look around. Tuners can be found cruising the streets around the world. They can also be seen taking center stage at competitions. Whipping around corners at high speeds, they impress judges and fans in drift races. Hundreds of tuner owners flock to the Battle of the Imports events each year. At these gatherings at U.S. racetracks, tuner owners compete head-to-head in drag races. Off the drag strip, they compete for prizes in huge car shows.

So what makes a tuner car? In short, a tuner car is a small passenger car that is customized, or "tuned," for better performance and looks. Builders often start with cars from Japanese manufacturers such as Toyota, Acura, and Subaru. From Mitsubishi Eclipses to Honda Civics, the options are almost endless for today's tuner car builders.

The neon green paint job on this Nissan Silvia helps it stand out in a crowd.

The Fast and the Furious *movie featured many tuner cars, such as the BMW M5 (front).*

TUNER CAR HISTORY

The history of tuner cars is fairly short. Before the 1970s, most Americans drove large cars built in the United States. These cars had big engines that used a lot of fuel. But in 1973, fuel prices soared. To save money, many Americans bought smaller cars from Japanese and European manufacturers. The foreign cars, or imports, used less gas than the American-made cars. Nobody knew it then, but imports would soon start a car craze all their own.

As demand for smaller cars grew, Japanese manufacturers began shipping their cars to the United States.

GETTING GREASY

By the early 1980s, the stage was set for tuner cars to make their appearance. Like "hot rodders" who tuned up older cars, some import owners wanted their cars to perform better. They also wanted their cars to show their personal style. Japanese Americans living in Southern California were some of the first to customize their imports. They made their cars lighter and faster. For better handling, they added **spoilers** and improved their cars' **suspension systems**.

But while performance was key, import owners didn't let their cars' looks go unnoticed. They replaced the wheels and added black tint to their windows. Some owners even painted flames or other designs on their car bodies. These tuned-up imports became known as tuner cars, or tuners.

Fast Fact: A person who builds a tuner car is also known as a tuner.

spoiler—a winglike device on the back of a car that forces air downward to help keep the car from lifting

suspension system—a system of springs and shock absorbers that soften a vehicle's up-and-down movements

9

The Datsun 510 was one of the first popular tuner cars. Eventually, more than half a million of these box-shaped cars sold worldwide. Datsun is now known as Nissan. The company continues to make cars that are popular with tuner builders. The Toyota Supra and the Mazda RX-3 also became popular with early tuner enthusiasts.

Some early tuner builders worked across car brands, or makes. These builders enjoyed an advantage—the parts were often interchangeable. This flexibility allowed early tuner owners to trade parts.

The light weight of the Datsun 510 helped make it a hit with tuner car builders. It weighed slightly more than 2,000 pounds (907 kilograms).

TUNERS VS. MUSCLE CARS

Early tuners were often compared to their souped-up American cousins known as muscle cars. Both types of cars had performance improvements. But most similarities ended there.

Muscle cars were made by companies such as Ford, Chevrolet, and Dodge. They had powerful eight-**cylinder** engines. They also had large, heavy frames. With this design, muscle cars reached high speeds quickly while traveling in a straight line.

Tuners were designed to be lightweight and **efficient**. Instead of large engines, they had smaller four- or six-cylinder engines. These engines produced less power than muscle-car engines did. But because tuners weighed less, they didn't need as much power to gain speed quickly. Their lighter weight also gave them better handling around curves.

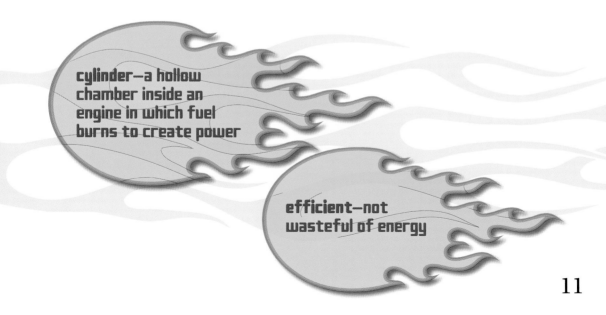

cylinder—a hollow chamber inside an engine in which fuel burns to create power

efficient—not wasteful of energy

11

In the mid-1980s, professional rally car racing spilled over into the tuner car movement. Rally racers added **superchargers** and **turbochargers** to their car engines to boost horsepower. Tuner car builders copied the look and performance of these rally cars.

By the late 1990s, it was clear that tuner cars were more than a fad. Tuner owners entered their cars in car shows. Some competed at the Battle of the Imports drag races held throughout the United States. Popular tuner models included the Honda Civic CX and CRX, the Mitsubishi GS-T Spyder, and the Mazda RX-7.

The 1997 video game *Gran Turismo* also helped increase interest in tuner cars. This Sony PlayStation game allows players to change the look and performance of imports. Players then "race" their tuner cars.

supercharger—a device that uses a belt or chain from the engine's crankshaft to force more fuel and air into the engine

turbocharger—a device that uses waste gases from a car's engine to spin a fan; the fan forces more fuel and air into the engine

In 2001, the movie *The Fast and the Furious* brought tuner popularity to new heights. The action movie featured tuners in wild street races. Street racing is against the law and very dangerous. Some tuner builders worried that the movie's racing scenes would make them look careless. But the movie had put tuner cars in the spotlight, and there was no turning back. Moviegoers everywhere wanted tuner cars of their own.

Fast Fact: A group called Tuners Against Street Racing sets up events to keep racing on official racetracks instead of the streets.

The Honda S2000 (front) was just one of the Honda models in *The Fast and the Furious* movie. The Honda Civic was also featured.

3 DESIGNING A TUNER CAR

Tuner cars are built by adding new parts and making changes to existing parts. Car owners spend months or years customizing their one-of-a-kind creations.

Tuners are so popular now that some manufacturers even give builders a head start. Some models of the Mitsubishi Lancer Evolution and the Subaru Impreza STI have turbochargers put in at the factory.

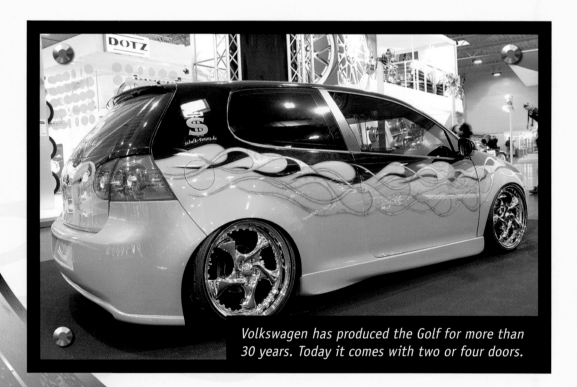

Volkswagen has produced the Golf for more than 30 years. Today it comes with two or four doors.

Today's most popular tuner cars include the Nissan Skyline, the Mazda RX-8, the Volkswagen Golf, and the Honda Civic Si. American companies have also joined foreign manufacturers in making smaller, more efficient cars. Ford, Pontiac, Dodge, and Chevrolet have all built cars that tuner builders like to use. These cars include the Ford Focus, the Dodge SRT, and the Pontiac Solstice.

The Ford Focus became a popular tuner model soon after its release in 2000.

Fast Fact: Companies such as Alpine Electronics have built tuner cars. They use the cars to help advertise their products.

Increasing horsepower is usually a tuner builder's main focus. One way to boost horsepower is to add more air and fuel to the engine. To do that, builders often add a supercharger or a turbocharger to their cars' engines. On average, a supercharger adds about 45 percent more horsepower to an engine. But much larger increases are possible. Turbochargers can increase horsepower by similar amounts. However, there is a slight delay in power delivery. The exhaust gases need to build up to provide power to the fan.

At car shows, tuner owners open their car hoods to display engine upgrades.

Nitrous oxide kits and cold-air intakes are two other devices that boost horsepower. Nitrous is made of chemicals that make more oxygen available to the engine. A cold-air intake brings in air from outside. The outside air is cooler because it isn't directly near the hot engine. This cooler air helps the fuel and air mixture burn.

Nitrous tanks are often placed in the backseat. Most tanks hold enough nitrous oxide to last a couple of minutes. Drivers press a button to deliver the gas to the engine.

TRANSMISSION TWEAKS

A transmission, or gearbox, transfers power from the engine to the drive wheels. Most tuners have manual transmissions. Unlike automatic transmissions, these gearboxes require the driver to change gears. Drivers shift gears using a lever called a stick shift. The shifting is often done in an "H" pattern.

Stainless steel shift-lever knobs add weight to the lever, which can make shifting faster.

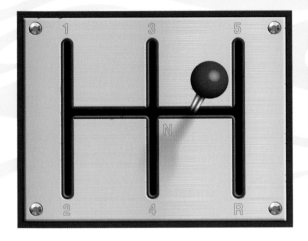

1-5 = 1st through 5th gear

R = Reverse

N = Neutral

* In the neutral position, no gear is selected. The car's tires roll freely.

No power is produced in the brief moment between gear shifts. The best way to maintain power is to reduce the time between shifts. For this reason, tuner owners often use sequential transmissions. With these gearboxes, drivers move the shift lever up and down in a straight line. Sequential shifters also make it impossible to accidentally skip gears. Skipping a gear can cause a loss of power to the engine.

Fast Fact: Some tuner builders shorten, or "chop," the shift lever to try to save shifting time.

SUSPENSION SYSTEM

Upgraded suspension systems are another "must-have" item for most tuner builders. These upgrades improve a car's handling around turns. Builders replace the front strut bars on the upper **chassis**. They replace the front tie bar on the lower chassis. Shock absorbers are upgraded to coil-over models for even firmer support. Some builders lower the chassis to prevent tilting around corners, or body roll. Adding a rear sway bar also helps prevent body roll.

Countless wheel designs are available, such as this six-spoke design.

chassis—the frame, wheels, axles, and parts that hold the engine of a car

Replacing the wheels is another common tuner upgrade. Builders who compete with their cars often use light, strong aluminum alloy wheels. Tuner builders looking for style often prefer shiny chrome wheels. The design and the number of **spokes** on the wheels varies. There can be as few as four spokes or more than 12.

A standard car tire is about 15 inches (38 centimeters) tall. But most tuner builders like the look of larger tires. Some tuner tires are more than 22 inches (56 cm) tall. Tuner builders also often use very wide tires. Wider tires have more contact with the road, providing better grip. A few racers even use racing slicks. The smooth outer surface of these tires helps them grip the track.

Fast Fact: Tuner car builders also consider the tread pattern of their tires. Fewer grooves help provide better handling. Some tires have fibers under the tread for extra strength.

spoke—one of the rods that connects the wheel rim to the center hub

No car is complete without the finishing touches. Some builders install custom doors. Lambo doors open straight up and down instead of to the side. Gullwing doors open by rising upward, the way a bird lifts its wings. Builders also make their cars stand out with custom paint jobs or vinyl graphic kits. Custom taillights and side markers are other popular additions.

Inside the cars, custom bucket seats provide style and comfort. Custom **gauges** are displayed on dash panels. High-tech speakers and stereo systems make the cars thump.

Lambo doors are sometimes called butterfly doors.

gauge—an instrument for measuring something, such as oil pressure

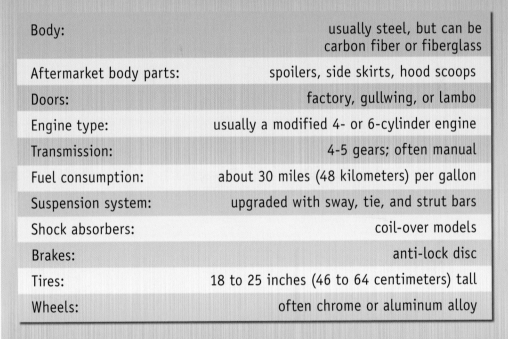

Tuner Cars at a Glance

Body:	usually steel, but can be carbon fiber or fiberglass
Aftermarket body parts:	spoilers, side skirts, hood scoops
Doors:	factory, gullwing, or lambo
Engine type:	usually a modified 4- or 6-cylinder engine
Transmission:	4-5 gears; often manual
Fuel consumption:	about 30 miles (48 kilometers) per gallon
Suspension system:	upgraded with sway, tie, and strut bars
Shock absorbers:	coil-over models
Brakes:	anti-lock disc
Tires:	18 to 25 inches (46 to 64 centimeters) tall
Wheels:	often chrome or aluminum alloy

Fast Fact: Some people install gaming equipment in their cars so that passengers can play video games.

4 TUNED FOR COMPETITION

Whether it's seen or heard going by, a tuner gets noticed. And that's part of the fun. Owners enjoy showing off their cars. They meet on side streets or in parking lots in a practice known as "posing." They enter their cars in shows and drive their lightweight, speedy cars in competitions.

Shows geared toward tuner car fans have become more popular since the early 2000s.

CAR SHOWS

As tuner cars became popular, car shows geared toward them did too. Today, hundreds of tuner owners enter their cars in the Battle of the Imports car shows. They compete for giant 6-foot (1.8-meter) trophies in several classes. The show also includes manufacturer awards for the best overall car of a certain make.

Since the late 1990s, thousands of tuner fans have visited the Hot Import Nights car shows around the United States. From Honda Civics to Mitsubishi Eclipses, every car gets its chance to shine under the lights.

For years, the Atlanta Motor Speedway in Georgia has hosted one of the largest car shows in the United States. Now known as the Motorsport Nationals, car owners compete for more than 600 prizes.

Each year, auto industry leaders flock to Las Vegas, Nevada, for the Specialty Equipment Market Association (SEMA) show. This show highlights the newest, most high-tech custom automobile parts available. The parts are featured in 12 categories. Along with vehicle parts, exhibitors display custom rides. Of course, tuners are always crowd favorites.

DRIFTING RACES

Drifting races started in Japan, but now they excite fans around the world. In these races, cars **powerslide** around the corners of a paved track to earn points from judges. In the first of two sessions, cars compete one at a time. Points are awarded for staying near the **line**, maintaining speed, and entering the corners at the best angle. Driving close to the track wall and getting an explosive crowd reaction also rack up points. In the second session, cars go two at a time. Points are awarded again, and the chasing car usually wins if it catches the lead car.

powerslide—to slide out of a turn by allowing the tires to lose their grip on the road

line—the marked path a drift racer should take on a course

Tire smoke trails behind two professional drift cars at a 2009 competition in Long Beach, California

Keiichi Tsuchiya

Keiichi Tsuchiya of Japan is considered the first great drift racer. Tsuchiya started racing professionally in the 1970s. He soon won several championships, earning him the nickname "Drift King." Tsuchiya is now retired from pro racing. But he continues to judge drifting competitions in Japan.

Fast Fact: Drift car tires produce smoke as they skid around turns. The Kumho Tire Company makes special tires that produce red, blue, or yellow smoke.

Drag races give tuner owners a chance to test the power of their cars safely.

While car shows and drifting have many fans, tuners take part in other competitions. Since 1990, tuners have been competing in the Battle of the Imports drag racing series. The fastest tuners in drag racing reach speeds of more than 190 miles (300 kilometers) per hour.

Other tuner owners enjoy winding through autocross courses. In these timed events, drivers compete one at a time on short courses marked by cones. Drivers receive time penalties for hitting the cones.

TUNER PRIDE

Whether zipping down racetracks or cruising the streets, tuner car owners take pride in their creations. Builders put a lot of thought into even the tiniest details of their cars. They want a car that perfectly suits them. That's what building tuners has always been about—the freedom to build your own dream machine.

Tuner car owners display their cars at a show in Long Beach, California.

GLOSSARY

alloy (A-loy)—a mixture of two or more metals

chassis (CHA-see)—the frame, wheels, axles, and parts that hold the engine of a car

chrome (KROHM)—a coating of a metallic substance called chromium

customize (KUHS-tuh-myz)—to change a vehicle based on the owner's needs and tastes

cylinder (SI-luhn-duhr)—a hollow area inside an engine in which fuel burns to create power

efficient (uh-FI-shuhnt)—not wasteful of time or energy

gauge (GAYJ)—an instrument for measuring something, such as oil pressure

line (LINE)—the marked path a drift racer should take on a course

powerslide (POW-ur-slide)—to slide out of a turn by allowing the tires to lose their grip on the road

spoiler (SPOI-lur)—a winglike device attached to the back of a car that directs air downward for better rear-tire grip

spoke (SPOKE)—one of the rods that connects the wheel's rim to the center hub

supercharger (SOO-pur-charj-ur)—a system that uses a belt or chain from the engine's crankshaft to force more fuel and air into the engine

suspension system (suh-SPEN-shuhn SISS-tuhm)—a system of springs and shock absorbers that soften a car's up-and-down movements

turbocharger (TUR-boh-charj-ur)—a device that uses waste gases from a car's engine to spin a fan; the fan forces more fuel and air into the engine

READ MORE

Doeden, Matt. *Custom Cars.* Motor Mania. Minneapolis: Lerner Publications Company, 2008.

McCollum, Sean. *Custom Cars: The Ins and Outs of Tuners, Hot Rods, and Other Muscle Cars.* RPM. Mankato, Minn.: Capstone Press, 2010.

Woods, Bob. *Wild Racers.* Racing Mania. New York: Marshall Cavendish Benchmark, 2010.

INTERNET SITES

FactHound offers a safe, fun way to find Internet sites related to this book. All of the sites on FactHound have been researched by our staff.

Here's all you do:

Visit *www.facthound.com*

FactHound will fetch the best sites for you!

Index